KNOWLEDGE ENCYCLOPEDIA

MODERN ART

© Wonder House Books 2022

All rights reserved. No part of this book may be reproduced or transmitted in any form by any means, electronic or mechanical, including photocopying and recording, or by any information storage and retrieval system except as may be expressly permitted in writing by the publisher.

(An imprint of Prakash Books)

contact@wonderhousebooks.com

Disclaimer: The information contained in this encyclopedia has been collated with inputs from subject experts. All information contained herein is true to the best of the Publisher's knowledge.

ISBN : 9789390391721

Table of Contents

Pre-Modern and Modern Art	3
Baroque Art	4–5
Rubens (1577–1640)	6–7
The Dutch Golden Age	8–9
Rembrandt (1606–1669)	10–11
Rococo Art	12–13
Neoclassical Art	14–15
Romanticism	16–17
Romanticism in Landscapes	18–19
The Pre-Raphaelites	20–21
Realism	22–23
Impressionism	24–25
Post-Impressionist Art	26–27
Van Gogh (1853–1890)	28–29
Symbolism	30–31
Word Check	32

PRE-MODERN AND MODERN ART

As we get closer to modern times, art history becomes more complex. The advancements of the modern period made it easier to travel and exchange materials and ideas. Thus, we find artists exploring different styles of art over their lifetime. They are no longer limited to a single period. Pablo Picasso, for instance, is considered to be one of the founders of Cubism. Yet, he also painted Neoclassical and Surreal pieces. Many of the artists mentioned in this book similarly experimented with different styles and mediums. Be sure to investigate the ones that catch your eye as you will be amazed by what you may discover!

▼ *The Old Guitarist (1903) and L'Aubade (1942) show two very different styles of modern art, executed by Picasso*

Baroque Art

Originating in Rome, baroque art bloomed over c.1590–1720. It rose in reaction to the strict rules of Renaissance art. It was also powered by the Catholic Church, which was trying to regain its influence over the western world. Baroque art is theatrical and stylistically complex. The works are dramatic, dynamic, and emotionally intense.

▲ St. Joseph the Carpenter (c. 1642) is a glowing piece of art by French baroque painter Georges de La Tour. Full of Christian symbolism, it shows a young Jesus with his earthly father, Joseph

Bernini's David

Baroque master Gian Lorenzo Bernini (1598–1680) captured a moment of biblical drama with *David*. As he prepares to catapult the fatal stone at his enemy Goliath, David is coiled with aggressive tension, his body twisted like a spring and his face furrowed in concentration. Only 24 years old at that time, Bernini broke the mould with this creation. Unlike previous self-contained sculptures of David—by Donatello and Michelangelo—Bernini's dynamic piece interacts with the space around it.

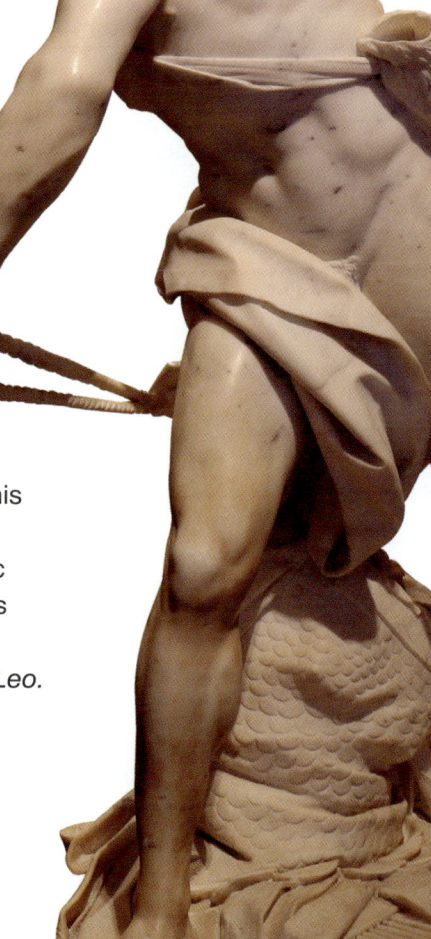

◀ The life-size marble masterpiece David (1623–1624), by baroque architect and sculptor Gian Lorenzo Bernini

Alessandro Algardi

High baroque sculptor Alessandro Algardi (1598–1654) rivalled Bernini with his creations. One of his best-known works is the gigantic relief-sculpture at St. Peter's Basilica in Rome called the *Meeting of Attila and Pope Leo.*

◀ Algardi's dramatic Fuga d'Attila (1646–53) gave an immeasurable boost to the art of creating marble reliefs

Caravaggism

Although not a baroque painter himself, the Italian artist Caravaggio (1571–1610) had a huge impact on the movement. His techniques of **tenebrism** and **chiaroscuro** were widely copied by such baroque masters as Rembrandt and Diego Velázquez.

Artemisia Gentileschi (1593–c. 1653)

Influenced by Caravaggism, Artemisia Gentileschi became one of the most famous female baroque masters. She was the first female artist elected into the Academy of the Arts of Drawing in Florence. Her amazing biblical art can be seen in *Judith Beheading Holofernes* (1620). It was considered a high point in baroque art.

◀ The macabre biblical scene of Judith Beheading Holofernes (1614–1620) by Artemisia Gentileschi

Incredible Individuals

Among Gentileschi's notable female predecessors were the Renaissance artist Sofonisba Anguissola (1532–1625) and Mannerist master Barbara Longhi (1552–1638). The portrait painter Lavinia Fontana (1552–1614) was the first woman to paint female nudes.

▶ Fontana's Minerva Dressing (1613) shows the Roman Goddess of wisdom and war

The Surrender of Breda

Diego Velázquez (1599–1660), court painter to King Philip IV, dominated Spanish baroque art. His *The Surrender of Breda* marks the military victory of his friend, the famed Spanish General Don Ambrogio Spinola, over the city of Breda (in Holland). Magnanimous Spinola set honourable terms for the defeated party. The painting shows him dismounting from his horse and meeting the Dutch leader as an equal. This showed that Spain wished for friendship with the Dutch party. Commissioned by the king in 1635, the painting was one of 12 battle scenes meant to decorate the throne room of the Buen Retiro Palace.

▲ The Surrender of Breda, c. 1635

Francisco de Zurbarán (1598–1664)

The devout Zurbarán painted serious, intense images influenced by Quietism, which is a Catholic movement rooted in submissive silence and penitential tasks. Zurbarán's mystical paintings of Saint Francis of Assisi are his best-known works. His creations use the shadowy textures of Caravaggism but are tinged with positive light. This gives the paintings a reserved yet emphatic feel.

▶ St. Francis in Meditation (1632), a painting by Zurbarán

Rubens (1577–1640)

The Flemish master Peter Paul Rubens is considered to be the most important baroque artist of northern Europe. A devout Catholic, Rubens believed that kings ruled by divine right. In addition to these deep convictions, his undeniable talent, Classical scholarship, and consistent diplomacy made him a favourite with the powers of Europe. He was eagerly sought after by the Church and State alike to portray their causes. The bulk of Rubens's work is thus, religious, historical, and mythological. His paintings are amazing pieces of movement and colour.

▲ The Fall of Phaeton, c. 1604, shows Zeus punishing Phaeton with thunderbolts for stealing the chariot of the Sun God, while the Hours and Seasons cower in terror. The horses were inspired by the drawings of Renaissance artist Leonardo da Vinci

▲ The Fall of the Damned, c. 1620, depicts a scene from the Last Judgement according to the Gospel of Matthew: Depart from me, ye cursed, into the eternal fire that is prepared for the devil and his angels

Samson and Delilah

A deceptively peaceful work, Rubens's *Samson and Delilah* shows yet another biblical tale. It depicts the Jewish hero Samson in deep sleep. The woman he loves, Delilah, has brought in servants to cut off his hair. Samson's hair is the source of his extraordinary strength. Without his hair, he would be easily captured by his enemies—the Philistine soldiers lurking behind the door. Rubens's painting is full of symbols. A statue of Venus and Cupid, the gods of love, stands in a corner. They indicate that love will be the cause of Samson's destruction. The barber's hands are crossed, representing deceit. Despite the large resting man in the centre, the scene is full of tension created by the masterful play of shadows and light.

▲ Rubens's Samson and Delilah (1609–1610) is an oil sketch on a wood panel. Another version of it exists as an ink-and-wash drawing on paper. The old woman behind Delilah is not part of the Bible story. She is thought to symbolise Delilah's grim future

Incredible Individuals

Experts believe that Samson's amazing physique here was inspired by Michelangelo's work, specifically the fresco of God creating Adam, painted on the ceiling of the Sistine Chapel.

The Marie de' Medici Cycle

In 1621, Rubens undertook a series of 24 paintings on the life and glory of Queen Marie de' Medici, the widow of Henry IV of France and the country's effective ruler. The series was an immense undertaking and Rubens did full justice to the paintings. He produced rich, vibrant, and imaginative paintings that showed royalty being celebrated by courtiers and divine beings.

Mythological creatures such as cherubs and nymphs, zodiacal figures like Sagittarius and gods like the all-powerful Saturn and the wise Minerva lend epic poetry to the life of the Queen. In the first painting, the Fates foretell her birth; in another, the Graces guide her education. In *The Meeting of Marie de' Medici and Henry IV at Lyons*, the couple is shown as Jupiter and Juno, the king and queen of the Roman gods. The series could have easily been frivolous and even satirical. Yet, Rubens's robust and impeccable style, combined with his genuine belief in the divine, gives the series of paintings a real ceremony and lasting artistic grandeur.

▲ *Marie de' Medici disembarks at Marseilles, France. Fame trumpets her arrival while sea gods and nymphs rise in welcome*

▲ *The Meeting of Marie de' Medici and Henry IV at Lyon; the lions pulling the chariot are a pun on the city's name*

▲ *The Triumph of Juliers shows the only military engagement in which Marie de' Medici took an active part*

▲ *The Coronation in Saint-Denis shows Marie de' Medici being crowned. Her young son and heir, the future Louis XIII of France, stands between her and the cardinal with his back to the viewer. The winged figures of Abundance and Victory shower her with blessings and gold*

The Dutch Golden Age

Baroque-period Holland developed its own art traditions called Dutch Realism. Lasting over 1600–1680, it created the Golden Age of Dutch art. The Protestant artists here preferred everyday subjects to monumental religious themes. They painted landscapes, still life, and portraits using oil paints and **easels**. New schools of art sprang up in towns like Haarlem, Delft, and Amsterdam. The Dutch Golden Age was enormously successful and deeply influenced later Impressionist painters such as Manet and Vincent van Gogh.

▲ *Cook at a Kitchen Table with Dead Game, c. 1634–1637, by Flemish artist Frans Snyders, who powerfully depicted still life and animal subjects in the Dutch Realist style*

▲ *The Bull by Dutchman Paulus Potter used a large canvas for a subject that was neither epic nor historical. Instead, it was sublimely rustic*

Jacob van Ruisdael (1628–1682)

One of the most gifted baroque masters, Ruisdael completed his first mature painting before he turned 20. Over 1650–1670, he painted innumerable landscapes, from views of Haarlem and changing seasons to woodlands, fields, countrysides, and dramatic seascapes. Ruisdael expressed the cyclical changes in the world. His canvasses reflect the mystical wonder of growth, decay, and the renewal of life. This is best seen in the *Jewish Cemetery*, where a dark scene of tombs, ruins, and gnarled old trunks contrasts with a rainbow and new greenery. Dense clouds, both grey and light, roll over the solemn scene, suggesting movement and change.

◀ *The Jewish Cemetery, c. 1654–1655*

In Real Life

Ruisdael's genius was rarely acknowledged in his lifetime. In 1681, the council of Haarlem was petitioned to allow him into the almshouse for the poor. He died there the following year. As fate would have it, his works fetch millions of dollars today!

MODERN ART

Jan Steen (1629–1679)

No baroque painter has portrayed the relations between children and grown-ups with such charm as Jan Steen. The artist's compositions show great humour and insight. He was sometimes so focused on the subject and expression that he became more of a cartoonist than a painter. Steen's works offer a moral and satirical look into the life of ordinary of his time.

▶ The World Turned Upside Down (c. 1663), is a typical Jan Steen picture showing the household at play while the housewife sleeps

Frans Hals (1582–1666)

The Flemish-born painter Frans Hals was a master portraitist, considered second only to Rembrandt. *The Laughing Cavalier* is his best-known work. Unlike most traditional portraits, which were stiff or serious, this one is imbued with the true presence of the subject. There is an informal lightness to the portrait that sets Hals apart from his fellow artists. *The Meagre Company* is one of his famous military group portraits. However, the painting was completed by the Amsterdam painter Pieter Codde. It is believed that Hals worked on the figures to the right, while Codde finished the group to the left.

▲ The Meagre Company, completed in 1637, shows militiamen carrying banners and lances

▲ Frans Hals's, The Laughing Cavalier (1624) is an iconic baroque portrait

Girl with a Pearl Earring

Painted by the brilliant Johannes Vermeer (1632–1675), the *Mona Lisa* of the North is a *tronie*, meaning 'face' in 17th-century Dutch. These paintings depicted people with exaggerated expressions or flamboyant costumes. Set in a dark background, the brightly lit girl gazes directly and softly at the viewer. Her expression and the mystery behind her identity has led people to compare this painting to the *Mona Lisa*. Vermeer has used his expertise in representing light to create her form rather than using lines. Vermeer made generous use of ultramarine blue, an expensive colour extracted from the semi-precious stone *lapis lazuli*.

▶ Girl with a Pearl Earring, c. 1665

Rembrandt (1606–1669)

The amazing Rembrandt Harmenszoon van Rijn was a supreme portrait artist and a master of Dutch Realism. He worked on a number of subjects and experimented with many styles. The resulting canvases were wondrous and deeply influenced far-off artists of the period, even though Rembrandt himself never travelled abroad. Rembrandt's prints, allegories, biblical art, and mythological paintings are particularly fine. He also gives us a clear idea of life as it was in 17th-century Amsterdam.

▲ The Blinding of Samson is a 1636 painting showing a key moment from the Bible when Samson is blinded by the Philistines

▲ One of the greatest paintings from Rembrandt's later years is the sorrowful Suicide of Lucretia, illustrating the event that led to the overthrow of the Roman monarchy and the establishment of the Republic of Rome

Painting Methods

Like many artists of his time, Rembrandt was influenced by Caravaggio's style. His own paintings were done with thick, broad brushstrokes and used layers of colours for intensity. His mastery over *chiaroscuro* is visible in the portraits and self-portraits. His paintings show both restraint and devotion, typical of Dutch Protestants.

▶ Self-Portrait with Beret and Turned-Up Collar, 1659

The Anatomy Lesson of Doctor Nicolaes Tulp (1632)

A landmark piece in guild portraits, *The Anatomy Lesson of Doctor Nicolaes Tulp* is a striking picture that was commissioned by the Amsterdam Guild of Surgeons. It shows the learned anatomist Dr Tulp dissecting the forearm of a cadaver. He is lecturing the other doctors on how muscles work. Rembrandt broke tradition while drafting this scene. Instead of painting the members grouped around the corpse and looking straight back at the viewer, he chose to portray an actual lesson. Thus, Dr Tulp is clearly speaking to his colleagues. The members look to him and at the corpse with clear interest. The lively composition established the reputation of the 26-year-old Rembrandt as a unique portraitist.

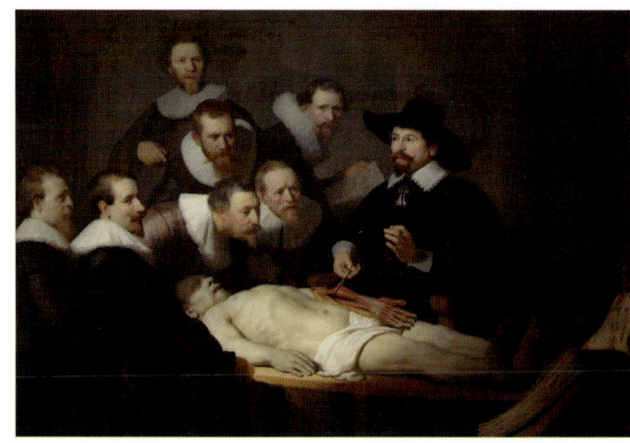

▶ The Anatomy Lesson of Doctor Nicolaes Tulp, 1632

MODERN ART

The Night Watch (1642)

Another piece that broke the mould was Rembrandt's painting called *The Night Watch*. Militia companies were usually drawn in neat rows, sitting, or standing. Rembrandt painted this militia with all of its equipment in hand, as if the members were waiting for orders to act. The artist uses *tenebrism* and fluid poses to suggest lively activity. The painting caused a lot of debate by turning an ordinary subject into a dynamic artwork. For a long time, a layer of varnish covered this piece, leading many to think—incorrectly—that the painting was a night scene.

▲ The Night Watch (1642), painted by Rembrandt at the height of his career

In Real Life

The amazing *The Storm on the Sea of Galilee* illustrates a biblical tale of Christ teaching his disciples the value of faith in the midst of a deadly storm. In 1990, this priceless treasure was stolen by two thieves who broke into the museum dressed as policemen. To this day, the museum has kept its original frame empty, waiting for the return of the painting.

▲ The Storm on the Sea of Galilee (1633)

Incredible Individuals

Within weeks of completing *The Night Watch*, Rembrandt lost his wife and muse, the heiress Saskia van Uylenborch. He was left with an infant son and a large house cluttered with his extravagant purchases. By 1656, he was bankrupt. Many religious pictures mark this troubled period. *The Supper at Emmaus* expresses the translucent gloom that both veils and reveals Rembrandt's figures in a deeply spiritual manner.

▶ The Supper at Emmaus (1648) depicts the story of Jesus after his crucifixion. The scene shows a resurrected Christ breaking bread with two disciples who have only just realised who he is

▲ Portrait of Saskia van Uylenburgh, c. 1634–1640

▲ Rembrandt painted his son Titus as a monk in 1660

Rococo Art

Under the patronage of King Louis XV (1710–1774) and his mistress Madame de Pompadour, a new art movement developed in France. This light-hearted, even frivolous style became popular in all forms of decorative art—from painting and sculpture to furniture and porcelain. Whimsical, mischievous, and elaborately decorative, it is called the Rococo style.

▲ *The work of French furniture maker Charles Cressent (1685–1768), this Rococo chest of drawers was created using rich woods, decorative gilt-bronze mounts, and a marble top*

Rococo Artists

Notable figures in Rococo art include Jean-Antoine Watteau (1684–1721), who was famous for his outdoor courtship scenes; Jean-Honoré Fragonard (1732–1806), who painted pictures of love; and Francois Boucher (1703–1770), who was known for his opulent, self-indulgent paintings.

From Venice, Giovanni Battista Tiepolo (1696–1770) earned his fame painting the fabulous frescoes at Würzburg Residence over 1750–1753. The nymph and satyr sculptures of Claude Michel Clodion (1738–1814) belong to this period. Clodion is also remembered as a sculptor of the relief on the Arc de Triomphe du Carrousel. In Britain, Thomas Gainsborough (1727–1788) achieved Rococo excellence in female portraits.

▶ *The Swing (1767), by Jean-Honoré Fragonard, is a typically mischievous Rococo painting of a young man peeking up at a woman while she swings high and sends her skirts and shoe flying into the air*

The Pilgrimage to Cythera

An **allegory** of falling in love, the *Pilgrimage to Cythera* belonged to a new genre of painting called the *fête galante*, which displayed playful outdoor gatherings. The painting expresses the elegant courtliness fashionable in Louis XV's France. In Classical mythology, Cythera is the birthplace of Venus, the goddess of love. Watteau's painting shows young people who have sailed to Cythera to find love. Some believe that the lovers have already met and are about to leave Cythera and return home. The entire painting has a wavy, rhythmic structure that conveys liveliness. The dreamy atmosphere, the peeping statue of Venus, the flying cherubs, all combine in beautiful contrasting shades to make this a Rococo masterpiece.

▲ *Pilgrimage to Cythera, c. 1717 by Jean-Antoine Watteau*

MODERN ART

Elisabeth Vigée Le Brun (1755–1842)

Completely self-taught, the gifted Elisabeth Vigée Le Brun became the court portraitist to Queen Marie-Antoinette of France. At a time when it was hard for women to become professional artists, Le Brun was a huge success. Her best works are portraits of women, including herself. She painted with a gentle, flattering style, which made her popular with Europe's nobility. Le Brun painted towards the end of the Rococo period and soon abandoned the style to become one of the earliest Neoclassical artists.

Incredible Individuals

François Boucher painted mythological scenes, particularly nudes, with great wit and charm. The influential French philosopher Denis Diderot (1713–1784) said of him, 'That man is capable of everything—except the truth.'

▶ Boucher's 1756 portrait of Madame de Pompadour

▲ Elisabeth Vigée Le Brun's Self-portrait in a Straw Hat, 1782, has the lively, light colours of Rococo, and the composition and proportions of early Neoclassicism

The Blue Boy (c. 1770)

One of Britain's most influential landscape artists, Thomas Gainsborough was also a talented portrait painter. *The Blue Boy* shows a combination of both these styles. In the background, Gainsborough painted a moody sky and the dark, tree-covered slope of a mountain. The boy is drawn standing confidently in **contrapposto**. His shiny clothes are drawn in great detail. The painting is in fact a costume study. It shows the frilly attire and shoes popular among boys and girls of this time. In contrast are the feathered male hat and bold pose, which show that the boy is on the verge of becoming a man.

Reynold's Grand Style

Gainsborough's greatest rival was the talented portrait painter Sir Joshua Reynolds. Influenced by Dutch, Flemish, and Renaissance masters, Reynolds tried to further the grand style of painting using rich, harmonious compositions without unnecessary detail and distractions.

▶ The Countess of Harrington's 1778–1779 portrait displays an air of icy self-confidence and expresses the grand style of Joshua Reynolds

▲ The Blue Boy, c. 1770, is believed to be a portrait of Jonathan Buttall, the son of a wealthy hardware merchant

Neoclassical Art

Neoclassicism was the popular art form of Europe throughout the late 18th and early 19th centuries. This was the Age of Enlightenment when Europe looked for reason and order. It was naturally inspired by the kindred spirit of Ancient Greece and Ancient Rome. Neoclassicism also arose in reaction to the grandiose baroque and frivolous Rococo art forms. In contrast, Neoclassical paintings and sculptures were serious. They portrayed heroic and self-sacrificial figures from Greek and Roman legend, often in stern forms and sombre colours. The art was meant to convey the generation's high moral values.

▲ Le Triomphe de 1810 is a high relief sculpture created by the French artist Jean-Pierre Cortot (1787–1843) on the Arc de Triomphe in Paris

▲ A Neoclassical masterpiece, Oath of the Horatii (1784) by the celebrated painter Jacques-Louis David (1748–1825) shows a scene from a Roman tale, and expresses patriotism and self-sacrifice for one's nation

Anton Raphael Mengs (1728–1779)

Known as the German Raphael, the Rococo artist Mengs was a founding master of Neoclassical painting. He was a court painter in Saxony and Madrid. His contemporaries held him to be the greatest painter alive. Mengs worked largely on portraits. He also produced altarpieces, prayer items, and large frescos as seen in the Royal Palace of Madrid. Perhaps his most famous work is the fresco called Parnassus on the ballroom ceiling at Villa Albani, Rome.

◀ Mengs's Parnassus (1761), is a painting of the mythical Mount Parnassus, home of the Greek god Apollo, shown here surrounded by the Muses

Angelica Kauffman (1741–1807)

Another founder of Neoclassicism, Angelica Kauffman was acclaimed by scholars of her time. She became famous with her Rococo portraits but soon moved on to more Classical pieces. Her famous 1790 painting shows the goddess Venus convincing Queen Helen of Sparta to run away with Prince Paris of Troy. This event sparked the Trojan War narrated in Homer's Greek epic poem, *The Iliad*.

▲ *Venus inducing Helen to fall in love with Paris, made in 1790 by Angelica Kauffman*

In Real Life

In 1768, Angelica Kauffman and fellow artist Mary Moser became two of the founding members of the Royal Academy of Arts in London. Even though they set the academy with the men, women were excluded from it for the next hundred years. As a result, it lost great talents like the wartime painter Elizabeth Thompson (1846–1933).

In 1860, the academy accepted an application from the worthy L. Herford, not realising that she was a woman! Even as late as 1980, there were only eight women in the academy. In 2020, the Serbian artist Marina Abramovic will become the first woman to have a solo show across the main galleries of the academy.

▲ *An 1802 print of the Royal Academicians Assembled in their Council Chamber, to Adjudge the Medals to the Successful Students in Painting, Sculpture, Architecture, and Drawing*

Antonio Canova

The famous Neoclassical sculptor Antonio Canova worked for the Pope and for Napoleon's family. But his mythological-themed works are by far his best. Among them is the mesmerising *Psyche Revived by Cupid's Kiss*. In a Sleeping Beauty-like tale, Psyche falls into a deathlike state after inhaling some fumes from a flask she was asked to bring from the Underworld by Venus. The sculpture shows the moment when a winged Cupid, the god of love, revives Psyche with a kiss.

▼ *Psyche Revived by Cupid's Kiss, commissioned in 1787 and executed by Antonio Canova (1757–1822)*

John Flaxman (1755–1826)

Another leading sculptor, Flaxman was also a designer, draughtsman, and engraver. He is famous for his work with Wedgewood's Jasperware, a popular type of stoneware that was perfected in 1775. Flaxman's designs were inspired by the forms of Ancient Rome. His 1808 monument to Admiral Nelson, a hero of the Napoleonic wars, is a Neoclassical masterpiece.

▶ *Hercules in the Garden of the Hesperides, designed by John Flaxman for Wedgwood, c. 1785*

Romanticism

The earliest examples of Romanticism can be seen in the works of the Spanish master El Greco (1541–1614). However, the style only took root towards the end of the 18th century. Romanticism took the heroic character of Neoclassicism, combined it with a revolutionary spirit, and expressed it with deep emotion. It was greatly inspired by poetry and literature. Artists of this genre held lofty beliefs in the goodness of humanity, justice for all, and a return to nature. They placed such feelings above reason and intellect. As a result, their art was a personal expression. It was an individual response to life, humanity, and the supernatural.

▲ The Nightmare, an eerie painting by Swiss artist Henry Fuseli (1741–1825), was one of the earliest works of Romanticism

▲ The 1827 Death of Sardanapalus by French Romantic artist Eugène Delacroix (1798–1863) was inspired by Lord Byron's popular play on the tragic last king of Assyria

The Wanderer Above the Sea of Fog

The exceptionally talented Caspar David Friedrich (1774–1840) was a keen observer and painter of nature. He interpreted the natural world in deeply personal terms, reflecting a touch of the mysterious and the divine. His masterpiece of symbolism, *Wanderer Above the Sea of Fog,* shows a striking figure standing in contemplation at the top of a hill. Before him, the land is shrouded in a shifting fog. It is as if the man is mesmerised by his journey ahead, into an unknown future.

▲ Ossian Receiving the Ghosts of the French Heroes is a painting by early Romanticist Anne-Louis Girodet de Roussy, 1767–1824

▶ The Wanderer Above the Sea of Fog, c. 1818

Francisco Goya (1746–1828)

The Spanish artist Francisco José de Goya y Lucientes was a court painter to Charles III and Charles IV of Spain. A portrait artist and printmaker, he illustrated key historical events of the 18th and 19th centuries. His works are valued as an important part of pre-modern art. Some of Goya's most moving paintings are stamped with the violence that followed Napoleon's conquest of Spain. *The Third of May 1808* shows the execution of Spanish rebels who rose against the French troops. Its companion piece, *The Second of May 1808*, illustrates the actual uprising. This tribute to Spanish resistance has such emotional force, it is one of the lasting icons of anti-war art.

▲ *The Second of May 1808*, also called *The Charge of the Mamelukes*, depicts the Spanish people's rebellion against the occupying forces of France during the Peninsular War

▲ *The Third of May 1808* shows the merciless execution of Spanish rebels by Napoleon's soldiers

The Lady of Shalott

The English artist John William Waterhouse (1849–1917) brought literary masterpieces to life with his marvellous paintings. His artworks are marked by broad brushstrokes and blocks of colour. Waterhouse's Romantic style was influenced by the Pre-Raphaelite movement, especially in his choice of subjects. This is seen in his most famous painting, *The Lady of Shalott*.

Painted in 1888, it illustrates Alfred Tennyson's famous poem of the same name, which is based on a legend from the time of King Arthur. The painting shows the tragic Elaine of Astolat, who defies a curse to go in search of her beloved knight. In her boat are three candles symbolising her life. Two of them have gone out, indicating the lady's fast approaching doom.

◀ This 1888 *Lady of Shalott* is the earliest and most evocative of Waterhouse's three beautiful paintings on the same subject

Incredible Individuals

In 1793, Goya suffered a serious illness that made him completely deaf. It left him somewhat isolated and prone to dark moods. This period marks a change in his paintings, which henceforth express a darker form of Romanticism.

◀ *Courtyard with Lunatics* was painted in 1793–1794 at a time when Goya was turning deaf. He often heard voices in his head and worried that he was going mad

Romanticism in Landscapes

Until the advent of Romanticism, landscapes were largely used as backgrounds for historical or heroic subjects. At best, they showed a sentimental country life. Such calm scenes came from biblical traditions and ideas. All this changed drastically in the hands of Romantic artists. Caspar David Friedrich, the founder of German Romantic landscape painting, believed that 'the artist should not only paint what he sees before him, but also what he sees in himself'. Thus, Romantic landscapes use the forces of nature to represent one's inner turmoil.

▲ Combining biblical subjects with sweeping sceneries, the English painter John Martin (1789–1854) produced sensational and apocalyptic landscapes, such as The Great Day of His Wrath (1853). Human beings are typically small in this genre of painting

▲ Gothic ruins made for magnificent landscapes, such as this Interior of Lindisfarne Priory (1797) by Thomas Girtin. Once again, the living beings are a minute part of a grander subject

Trends in Landscape Painting

As attitudes towards landscape painting changed, artists began to portray wild, fluctuating sceneries, often with medieval buildings and ruins. This trend was first seen in English paintings from the latter half of the 18th century, with the works of such pioneers as Richard Wilson (1714–1782) and Thomas Girtin (1775–1802). Over the 19th century, different types of landscape art developed in the West. In Russia, it found expression through the *Peredvizhniki*, a group of artists nicknamed 'the Wanderers'. In America, the Hudson River School came to the forefront of landscape painting.

▲ The stark yet sublime style of Richard Wilson, the father of English landscape painting, can be seen in his c. 1765 painting of the lake Llyn-y-Cau on the Cader Idris mountain in Wales

▲ The Rooks Have Come Back (1871), painted by Alexei Savrasov (1830–1897), a member of the Wanderers, when he was at the height of his career

John Constable (1776–1837)

The son of a mill owner, John Constable grew up in an area of natural beauty. Blessed with keen observational powers, he expressed his appreciation of nature in evocative detail. Indeed, the Romantic painter Henry Fuseli once remarked that Constable's work 'makes me call for my greatcoat and umbrella'. Constable contributed greatly to English landscape painting, with such pieces as the incredibly lifelike painting *The Cornfield* (1826). This was inspired by James Thomson's poem *Summer*.

▶ *"A fresher gale begins to wave the woods and stir the streams, sweeping with shadowy gusts the fields of corn."*—Summer, James Thomson

The Hay Wain

One of Constable's most famous paintings, *The Hay Wain* (1821), was originally exhibited simply as *Landscape: Noon*. It captures the sunny, green nature of the English countryside in summer. It also represents the quiet contentment that Constable felt while surveying this familiar scene. The man in the painting is immersed in his surroundings, illustrating a Romantic belief of the relationship between nature and humanity.

▶ *The Hay Wain (1821) shows a scene on the River Stour and is one of Constable's most popular masterpieces*

The Battle of Trafalgar

Known as "the painter of light", John Mallord William Turner (1775–1851) is a celebrated master of English landscape painting. He had an entirely original way of mixing Romanticism and Realism, which inspired the spectacular Impressionist developments in landscape painting.

Unique among Turner's works is the *Battle of Trafalgar*. Under the command of Admiral Nelson, the battle established the supremacy of the English navy. Despite this victory, Turner's expression of military heroism focuses on chaos and death. The sea is turbulent with war. Ships clash and toss their men overboard. It shows the final moments of Admiral Nelson's tragic end.

◀ *The Battle of Trafalgar, painted 1822–1824*

The Pre-Raphaelites

Raphael was the most celebrated artist who lived and painted at the end of the Renaissance period. Over 300 years later, a group of British painters came together under his name. The founding members were three students of the Royal Academy of Arts—Dante Gabriel Rossetti, William Holman Hunt, and John Everett Millais. They were joined by others later on. Their aim was to return the arts to a time of higher inspiration. In 1848, the West was going through industrialisation. Photography was gaining popularity. The Pre-Raphaelites bemoaned the lack of imagination in the art of their times. Thus, they took inspiration from medieval sources like the legends of King Arthur, from Renaissance writers like Shakespeare, and from Romantic poets such as Keats.

▲ William Holman Hunt's 1868 painting titled Isabella and the Pot of Basil depicts a scene from a romantic and eerie poem by John Keats

▲ The Death of King Arthur, a tender medieval scene painted c. 1860 by James Archer (1823–1904)

Marie Spartali (1844–1927)

Being an artist in Victorian England was not considered a 'suitable occupation' for a woman. Marie Spartali Stillman was one of the few professional female artists in the latter half of the 19th century. She was very successful and had close ties with the Pre-Raphaelite circle. Her 1885 watercolour *Love's Messenger* shows a woman standing by an open window. A dove has just delivered a letter into her hands. There are symbols of love all about her; the red rose on her dress, the blindfolded Cupid, and even the dove itself.

▶ Love's Messenger, by Marie Spartali Stillman, painted with symbols that express love and beauty in full bloom

Dante Gabriel Rossetti (1828–1882)

One of 19th century's most influential painters was Dante Gabriel Rossetti. A gifted poet, writer, translator, and artist, he was perhaps the most remarkable leader of the Pre-Raphaelite Brotherhood. His paintings were perhaps not skilled in a technical way, but they were so amazingly imaginative that you could not tear your eyes away from them. Many of the subjects were inspired by literature and were done in both oil and watercolours. Rossetti also created illustrations for stained glass windows like the scene of Tristram and Ysoude drinking a love potion in a legend from the time of King Arthur. One of Rossetti's most famous works is the *Beata Beatrix*, a deeply personal painting of his artist-wife Elizabeth Siddal painted in the years after her death.

▲ *Sir Tristram and la Belle Ysoude drinking the love potion* is a stained-glass window illustrated by Dante Gabriel Rossetti. It is part of a set of 13 stained glass panels, of which Rossetti designed two

▲ *Beata Beatrix* (1864–1870) by Dante Gabriel Rossetti

In Real Life

Dante Gabriel Rossetti's paintings are so popular, you can buy them online as poster art. He is best known to children today as the illustrator of the *Goblin Market*, a story in verse by his sister Christina Rossetti.

▶ Sweet-toothed Laura pays for the goblin's wicked fruit with a lock of her golden hair, an illustration by Dante Gabriel Rossetti for the Goblin Market

Isn't It Amazing!

Many famous people actually found the works of the Pre-Raphaelites irreverent and blasphemous. Key among them was the greatest novelist of the Victorian era, Charles Dickens.

▲ John Everett Millais's brilliantly executed *Christ in the House of His Parents* (1849–1850) drew criticism from Charles Dickens, who thought the Virgin Mary had been depicted too hideously

Realism

Originating in France in the 1850s, Realism aimed at illustrating objective truth. It did away with supernatural elements and artificial exaggerations. Exotic subjects and artistic traditions were discarded. Instead, Realists tried to show gritty, everyday facts. They held up a mirror to the industrial and commercial nature of their times. French Realism, as founded by Honoré Daumier, Jean-François Millet, and Gustave Courbet, honoured the working classes and their environment.

▲ *The Birdcatcher, by Vasily Perov (1834–1882), who pioneered the new style of Critical Realism in Russian art*

▲ *Sad Inheritance (1899), by the Spanish artist Joaquín Sorolla y Bastida, is a striking painting of disabled children bathing in the sea. This style is known as Social Realism*

The Realism Exhibition

The term Realism had been floating around since the 1840s, but it really took off after an incident in 1855. During the World's Fair in Paris, the painter Gustave Courbet was prevented from displaying one of his works titled *The Painter's Studio*. Not one to be discouraged by such rejection, Courbet set up his own exhibition. He sent out flyers and invited people to view his personal exhibition. It was called 'Pavilion of Realism'.

Courbet was inspired by Rembrandt's *The Night Watch* and *The Anatomy Lesson* to pursue Realism. His painting, *A Burial at Ornans,* shows the funeral of his great-uncle in his hometown. Rather than using models for the painting—as was considered normal—Courbet painted the very people who had been present at the burial. Critics thought he was making his pictures unnecessarily ugly; the subject of a large funeral was normally reserved for very important people.

◀ *The Painter's Studio shows Courbet's friends, members of French society, and allegorical figures*

The Third-Class Carriage

The railways were a miracle of the Industrial Age. They fascinated Honoré Daumier (1808–1879), who sketched and painted the realities of this new mode of transportation. In *The Third-Class Carriage*, Daumier observes the cramped, dirty compartments that working-class Parisians were forced to travel in. He paints with sympathy, a family of women and children in the front row. The whole scene captures the plight of the people and a moment of quiet in their harried lives.

▲ *The Third-Class Carriage, c. 1862–1864, by Daumier*

The Gross Clinic

One of the best American Realist paintings ever created is *The Clinic of Dr Gross*, an 1875 masterpiece by the painter, photographer, and sculptor Thomas Eakins. The painting illustrates a lecture in modern surgery, given by the famous Philadelphia surgeon Dr Samuel Gross. Eakins paints this pioneering medical man in a severe yet heroic manner. He is upright, his forehead glows, and the blood on his hands catches the light as he pauses to explain the procedure.

Next to him, the mother of the patient covers her face in horror. The assistants are engrossed in the surgery. When the painting was exhibited, people did not know how to react. Indeed, the viewers may have found it morbid and criticised the artist, judging the detail to be too realistic. The work was even rejected by the Centennial Exhibition of 1876. Today, it is one of the most celebrated paintings in its genre.

▲ *The Gross Clinic (1875) by Thomas Eakins*

▶ *Incense of a New Church (1921), by Charles Demuth (1883–1935), demonstrates the Precisionist style. Sharp industrial smog and dark factories replaced the churches that once dominated the American landscape*

In Real Life

Courbet's painting *The Stonebreakers* (1849) is a sympathetic work showing the artist's concern for the difficulties of the poor. The canvas shows two men toiling under the sun, breaking and removing stones from a road that is under construction. The painting was destroyed in the bombing of Germany in WWII.

▲ *The Stonebreakers (1849) by Gustave Courbet*

Realism in the 20th Century

With a series of horrific wars, the **Great Depression** and the development of nuclear weapons, 20th century Realists had a plethora of subjects to choose from. Modern Realism thus, split into a wide variety of forms. For instance, the 1920s saw the rise of Precisionism in America. This style captured urban landscapes in sharp-focus realism.

Impressionism

During the late 1860s and early 1870s, Paris (and then France) saw the rise of Impressionism. This became one of the most influential pre-modern art movements. The name was coined in 1874 by Louis Leroy, a French art critic, after he saw Claude Monet's 1872 painting titled *Impression: Sunrise*. In its purest form, Impressionism advocates *plein-air* painting, which means painting outdoors. It is identified by rapid, loose brushstrokes, and the spontaneous application of paint. Impressionists tried to capture fleeting moments in light. A landscape that turned orange in the sunset would be painted orange. This non-natural depiction of light and swift brushwork made Impressionism a revolutionary movement in Western art.

▲ *Impression, soleil levant* (in English, *Sunrise*) by Claude Monet (1840–1926), one of the founders and most prolific artists of Impressionism

Camille Pissarro (1830–1903)

A father figure to many artists of his time, Camille Pissarro sought to depict nature in its myriad colours and changing tones. He was central to the Impressionist and Post-Impressionist movements and was often treated as a mentor and teacher. His first paintings in the genre shocked people. They were regarded as too muddy and too rustic. People were more used to heroic and mythological subjects. Pissarro's ways of using colour to show shadows and light was also considered revolutionary.

Alfred Sisley (1839–1899)

The 'forgotten Impressionist', Alfred Sisley was a master of *plein-air* painting. A skilled yet underestimated Impressionist, he painted natural landscapes. Though he was a British citizen, he spent most of his time in France capturing its countryside and waterways in open compositions and vivid colours. His work differs from other Impressionists in its thoughtful and balanced composition, and a gentle quietness that permeates each canvas.

▲ *Pont Boieldieu in Rouen, Rainy Weather* is an 1896 painting by Pissarro of a new iron bridge near the Gare d'Orléans train station and the Place Carnot square. Here, Pissarro moved beyond traditional rural landscapes to a busy industrial area; eventually depicting it in a number of paintings under different light and weather conditions

▲ *The Terrace at Saint-Germain, Spring* (1875) by Alfred Sisely

Édouard Manet (1832–1883)

Related to the French monarch, Manet was highly revered by Impressionist painters. By the age of 29, the precocious artist was already considered the movement's leading figure. Manet's mesmerising paintings captured the dynamic city life of Paris and the leisurely pastimes of its upper class. He painted bars, cafes, clubs, and races. He was also a noted portrait artist, reflecting the joys and the loneliness of urban people.

▲ An early painting, the 1862 Music in the Tuileries Gardens shows a fashionable crowd gathered at the famous Paris gardens for a concert. The painting includes portraits of Manet's friends and family

Edgar Degas (1834–1917)

Famous for his many, many paintings of ballet dancers, Edgar Degas was less focused on the effects of light and more interested in natural gestures and movements. His carefully balanced works offer a snapshot of his subjects' unguarded moments. Unlike other artists of Impressionism, he rarely attempted *plein-air* painting. Instead, he preferred to work at his studio producing amazing artworks with watercolours, sketches, pastels, and sculptures.

▲ Degas's ballet dancers seem poised to dance right out of the canvas

Paul Cézanne (1839–1906)

An important artist of Impressionism and Post-Impressionism, the French painter Paul Cézanne is revered as the "father of modern art". His developments in colour, composition, and perspective led the transition to 20th century art. His works are easily identified by their repetitive brushwork. The genius Pablo Picasso acknowledged him as "my one and only master".

▲ One of the five paintings in the series titled The Card Players, which marked the start of Cézanne's greatest period of art

Pierre-Auguste Renoir (1841–1919)

A master at portraying 'dappled light', Renoir was a genius painter of women, children, and nature. His *plein-air* painting vividly captures shifting lights. His earlier works are marked by dark colours and the heavy technique called **impasto**. After 1868, his colours became lighter and more natural. This was in part due to his work with fellow artist Monet.

▲ The Dance at Le Moulin de la Galette (1876), shows Renoir's incredible depiction of dappled afternoon light playing over the faces and clothes of the festive people

Post-Impressionist Art

Post-Impressionism is the general style of art that appeared during the 1880s and the 1890s. It was pioneered by the generation of artists who followed the Impressionists. They were not content with being restricted to nature and *plein-air* painting. They experimented widely with colour. The period saw the rise of many art movements such as Neo-Impressionism, early Expressionism, and Fauvism.

Whistler's Mother

The 1871 *Arrangement in Grey and Black No.1* is an iconic American painting popularly called *Whistler's Mother*. It is a portrait of Anna Matilda, the devout, strict mother of James Abbott McNeill Whistler (1834–1903). According to legend, she posed for this painting when one of Whistler's sitters failed to turn up. The artist, who avoided morality and sentimentality in his work (which is apparent from the title), painted Anna in austere shades. The brilliance of the work lies in its carefully balanced composition and shapes.

▶ *Arrangement in Grey and Black No.1 by James Whistler*

Neo-Impressionists

The **avant-garde** Neo-Impressionists refined the impulsive Impressionist movement with a special way of painting. Instead of mixing colours on a **palette** and applying it to the canvas, Neo-Impressionists dotted their colours directly on to the canvas. These groups of coloured points formed a coherent image in the mind of the viewer. This method is called Pointillist painting. It gives greater luminescence to pigments and a brilliance to the whole piece. Neo-Impressionism was founded by Georges Seurat (1859–1891) and his disciple Paul Signac (1863–1935).

Seurat's Pointillism

A Sunday Afternoon on the Island of La Grande Jatte (1884–1886) is the Georges Seurat masterpiece that kicked off the Neo-Impressionist movement. Look closely and you will notice the whole painting is a series of closely packed dots. Seurat went to the park every day at the same hour for months. He sketched the visitors, went back to his studio and transferred his observations onto the canvas. The people thus, seem isolated and silent.

◀ *A Sunday Afternoon on the Island of La Grande Jatte (1884–1886) by Seurat*

MODERN ART

Paul Signac

After the death of Seurat, the Post-Impressionist painter Paul Signac became the leader of the Neo-Impressionist art movement. Signac's work largely comprises vividly coloured landscapes and seascapes. He further developed Seurat's Pointillism. His experiments with different ways of applying colour influenced later schools of art, including Fauvism. His greatest pieces include *The Papal Palace, Avignon* (1900), and *Port of Marseilles* (1905).

▲ *The Port of Saint-Tropez (1901–1902) by Paul Signac*

Fauvism

A short-lived art movement, the highly fashionable Fauvism, was associated with a group of French artists between 1905 and 1907. Henri Matisse (1869–1954) and André Derain (1880–1954) were the leaders of this style. The word comes from the French term *les fauves*, meaning "the wild beasts". The style was characterised by wild brushwork, contrasting colours, and simplified figures. People were shocked by the paintings at first because they were unlike anything ever seen in the art world.

Japonism

Many French Impressionists and Post-Impressionists, from Monet to Vincent van Gogh, were influenced by Japanese art trends, especially by the woodblock prints of c.1600–1900 termed *ukiyo-e* (pictures of the floating world). The most influential works came from Hokusai (1760–1849) and Hiroshige (1797–1858).

▲ *Under the Wave off Kanagawa, c. 1830–1832, the most famous of Hokusai's prints, is the first of a series called Thirty-six Views of Mount Fuji. Notice the snow-clad mountain in the distance*

▲ *Vivid expressions using bright, unnatural colours mark the short-lived Fauvist style*

💡 Isn't It Amazing!

In 1885, the song-writing duo Gilbert and Sullivan lampooned British traditions and government in a comic opera set in fictional Japan. *The Mikado* has remained popular ever since.

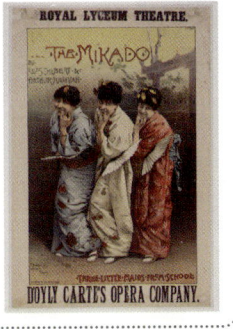

▶ *The 1885 poster announcing The Mikado shows its three heroines— Yum-Yum, Pitti-Sing, and Peep-Bo*

Van Gogh (1853–1890)

One of the most celebrated Post-Impressionists in the world today is the Dutch painter Vincent van Gogh. Van Gogh only painted during the last decade of his short life. But these proved to be prolific years, with the artist creating a new picture almost every four days. His energetic, almost frantic paintings reflected his life, and state of mind. From his vivid self-portraits, to the enthusiastically bright *Sunflowers* and many ominous landscapes, the paintings reflected the artist's days, the influence of his friends, his intense inner world, and his fading health.

▲ Van Gogh was influenced by Japanese art, as seen here in his 1887 oil painting The Courtesan (after Eisen). This specifically refers to the work of Japanese artist Kesai Eisen

▲ It is generally believed that Vincent sold only one painting during his lifetime—The Red Vineyard, painted in 1888 near Arles, France

The Early Style

Vincent first began drawing with pencils, charcoal sticks and watercolours. His early subjects were poor, hardworking people for whom he felt great sympathy. His early oil paintings also show similar subjects in dark, gritty colours. Most famous among them is *The Potato Eaters* (1885). This grim picture shows a peasant family at their frugal dinner. Their coarse and ugly faces were the result of several studies by van Gogh. However, most of his contemporaries were displeased with the unflattering realities it portrayed.

◀ The Potato Eaters (1885)

⭐ Incredible Individuals

As a young man, Vincent tried and failed at numerous jobs. He was a teacher, a minister, worked at a bookstore, an art gallery, and even became a missionary. He finally dedicated his life to art around the age of 27. He was supported by his brother Theo, who sent him money, encouragement, and even tried (unsuccessfully) to sell his paintings.

▶ Worn Out, an 1882 pencil sketch of a war veteran at a local almshouse

The Maturing Painter

Van Gogh moved to Paris in 1886 to live with his brother Theo and learn from the artists. Here, he was influenced by men such as Monet, Degas, Pissarro, and even became friends with Gauguin. Vincent learned to use bright colours and new techniques of brushwork. He practiced making portraits—even painting 20 self-portraits when he could find no other models!

In 1888, he found a house in Arles in sunny southern France, where he painted his vibrant, happy *Sunflowers* series. Van Gogh's paintings took on new intensity and emotion here. Not only did he choose more vibrant colours, he often applied paint directly from the tube to the canvas. He painted with such thick rough brush strokes that the paintings would take weeks to dry.

▶ After a heated confrontation with Paul Gauguin, during a mental breakdown, van Gogh cut off part of his left ear, wrapped it up and gave it to a woman for safekeeping. He later painted a self-portrait with his bandaged ear

▲ *Vase of Twelve Sunflowers (1888)*, part of a series painted in Arles. The second painting of the series was part of a Japanese collection and was destroyed in a fire during WWII

Fading Health

By 1889, van Gogh had become so moody, depressed and unpredictable, he committed himself to a mental hospital. He was no longer able to look after himself. Yet, he painted with vigour. Some of his most enduring works like the exquisite *Starry Night,* with its cypress trees and swirling colours, come from this period. In July 1890, he committed suicide by shooting himself in the chest.

▶ Van Gogh's mesmerising, swirling Starry Night illustrates a moonlit scene near the asylum where he stayed

▲ *Wheatfield with Crows (1890)*, often thought to be van Gogh's greatest and last artwork

Symbolism

A late 19th century Post-Impressionist movement, Symbolism flourished throughout Europe, particularly in German, French, and Belgian regions. It arose in literature and poetry and soon spread to other art forms. Symbolism had deep connections with the Pre-Raphaelites and Romanticism. In turn, it influenced Expressionism and Surrealism. Symbolism came about as a reaction against Realism and its gritty, objective focus. Instead, Symbolists chose mythological and fantastical subjects. They looked for the extraordinary. They searched for a deeper reality arising from their dreams and inner world.

▲ At the height of his Golden Period, Austrian artist Gustav Klimt painted The Kiss an oil painting covered in gold and silver leaf to symbolise the wonderfulness of love

Death of the Gravedigger

This lovely painting by the German painter Carlos Schwabe (1866–1926) is full of Symbolist motifs. The painting features a gravedigger digging his own grave, while the angel of death visits him. The gravedigger's face is peaceful even in death, while his soul (the green light) is taken away in the protective arms of the angel.

▲ 'The Knight at the Crossroads' (1882) by Victor Vasnetsov brings to life a Russian legend, The Three Journeys of Ilya Muromets. On a bleak landscape, the hero pauses over this stone inscription: 'If you go straight ahead, there will be no life; there is no way forward for he who travels past, walks past, or flies past'.

In Real Life

In 1989, Chinese troops gunned down students and civilians who were protesting for democracy at the Tiananmen Square in Beijing. This shocking massacre and the uncertain times that followed gave birth to protest paintings in a style called Cynical Realism. Chinese painters used Symbolist motifs to convey their message of irony and ridicule.

▲ Death of the Gravedigger (1895) by German painter Carlos Schwabe (1866–1926)

The Lady with the Pig

The best-known work of Félicien Rops (1833–1898), a Belgian artist and pioneer of Belgian comics, is titled *Pornocrates or The Lady with the Pig*. The pig here symbolises luxury and evil. It is misleading a woman, who follows with a blindfold over her eyes. They stand on a marble stage, below which are allegorical male figures of the arts like Sculpture, Music, Poetry and Painting. The fine arts seem to despair beneath the heels of decadence.

The Flying Carpet

One of the first artists to turn fantasies into paintings, Viktor Mikhaylovich Vasnetsov (1848–1926) caused a media storm with his *The Flying Carpet*. In this fairy tale picture, he expressed the Russian people's longing for a bright future. The hero soars freely in the bright open sky. He stands confidently, richly clothed, holding magical gifts like the large golden cage of a firebird. The carpet—an amazing vehicle—was also drawn for the sake of Savva Mamontov, the wealthy industrialist who commissioned the painting.

▲ *The Flying Carpet is Vasnetsov's 1880 depiction of Ivan Tsarevich, a hero from Russian folktales*

Incredible Individuals

One of the giants of Post-Impressionist Symbolism was the enigmatic painter Paul Gauguin (1848–1903). He developed a simplified, non-naturalistic style of painting to express his emotions. This is recognisable by his decorative line work, flat bold colours, and perplexing use of symbols. Tragically, few people appreciated his works while he was alive, and he died in poverty.

▲ *Gauguin's 1897–1898 painting titled Where Do We Come From? What Are We? Where Are We Going?*

Word Check

Allegory: It is the illustration of ideas and concepts like love, revolution, glory, etc., in the form of symbols and human figures.

Avant-garde: It is a French word for 'advance guard'; it refers to artists who are at the forefront of radical and ground-breaking new styles.

Chiaroscuro: It is a style of painting that contrasts dark and light colours, usually to enhance the three-dimensional effect of a painting.

Contrapposto: It is an Italian word that describes a human pose. It is when the figure stands with most of its body weight on one leg, while the other leg is free and bent a little at the knee. The upper part of the body is usually angled in a natural way.

Easels: They are the wooden frames that hold the artist's canvas.

Great Depression: It was a severe worldwide economic crisis in the 1930s that robbed people of their homes and their livelihood.

Impasto: It is a way of painting in which the paint is applied in such thick layers, with a brush or painting knife, that it sticks out of the canvas.

Palette: It is a board on which the painter can mix colours before applying them to the canvas.

Tenebrism: It is a style of painting developed by 17th-century Spanish and Italian painters (notably Caravaggio). It makes use of dark shadows to paint a picture while highlighting selected parts.